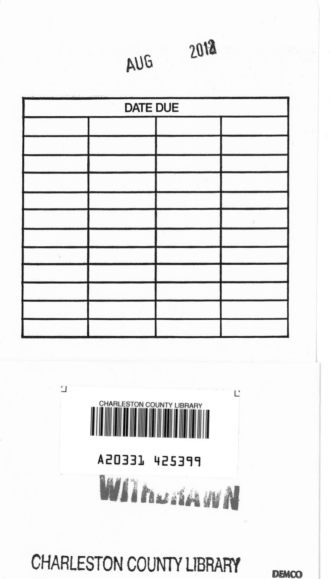

cloverleaf books™

Holidays and Special Days

Marco's Cinco de Mayo

Lisa Bullard

illustrated by Holli Conger

M MILLBROOK PRESS · MINNEAPOLIS

For Etta —L.B.
To CC, WC, and itty-bitty OC. Thank
you for allowing me to follow my
dreams. —H.C.

Millbrook Press
A division of Lerner Publishing Group, Inc.
241 First Avenue North
Minneapolis, MN 55401 U.S.A.

Website address: www.lernerbooks.com

Main body text set in Slappy Inline 18/28.
Typeface provided by T26.

Library of Congress Cataloging-in-Publication Data

Bullard, Lisa.
    Marco's Cinco de Mayo / by Lisa Bullard ; illustrated by Holli
Conger.
        p.   cm. — (Cloverleaf books. Holidays and special days)
    Includes index.
    ISBN 978-0-7613-5082-8 (lib. bdg. : alk. paper)
    1. Cinco de Mayo (Mexican holiday)—Juvenile literature.
2. Mexico—Social life and customs—Juvenile literature.
3. Cinco de Mayo, Battle of, Puebla, Mexico, 1862—Juvenile
literature. I. Conger, Holli, ill. II. Title.
F1233.B858 2012
972'.07—dc23   2011021293

Manufactured in the United States of America
1 – BP – 12/31/11

TABLE OF CONTENTS

That's a holiday that started in Mexico. People there speak Spanish. "Cinco de Mayo" means the **"5th of May"** in Spanish.

TACOS

UNITED STATES

MEXICO

Mexico is a neighbor of the United States. Many people have moved from Mexico to live in the United States. Many people in the United States have family members in Mexico.

My family is **Mexican American**.
We celebrate Cinco de Mayo here in the
United States too.

My city has a big parade. There are games, carnival rides, music, and dancing. The yummy Mexican food is the best part.

Cinco de Mayo celebrations are popular in many U.S. cities. You don't have to be Mexican American to go. The celebrations in the United States are bigger than most in Mexico.

Chapter Two

A Big Problem

This year, I haven't even had one taco.
I'm too nervous. I'm one of the dancers.
Lots of people are here to watch.

Dancers and other people wear costumes for Cinco de Mayo. The costumes are based on different times and places in Mexico's history.

What if I forget all the steps?

There's my cousin Diego!

He's the one who taught me this dance.

10

Last night, Diego told me a story. He said it would help if I felt afraid.

Chapter Three
Brave and Proud

Diego told me about the **first** Cinco de Mayo. It happened about 150 years ago.

France sent many soldiers to Mexico to start a **war**. People thought the French soldiers were the best in the world.

Spain ruled Mexico for hundreds of years. The Mexicans fought a war to be free from Spain from 1810 to 1821. When the French soldiers came in 1861, the Mexicans got worried. They did not want to lose their freedom again.

13

The Mexican army was small. But the Mexicans were **brave and proud** of their country.

On May 5, 1862, they did something surprising.

They **won** a big battle against the French soldiers!

The May 5th battle did not end Mexico's war with France. But the Mexican people remembered Cinco de Mayo. They kept fighting. Finally, they won.

I can be brave and proud too. I listen to the **mariachi band** while I wait to go onstage.

Mariachi music has been popular in Mexico for a long time. Mariachi bands use instruments like violins, guitars, and trumpets. The band members wear fancy costumes.

Suddenly my feet are ready to dance!

Chapter Four

The Taco Battle

Diego says I did a great job dancing. It sure made me hungry. We have a **taco-eating battle.** I eat two more than Diego!

Tacos are made from tortillas wrapped around a filling. Tortillas are Mexican bread. They are flat, thin, and round.

Boom! The fireworks flash the colors of the
Mexican flag. Cinco de Mayo is almost over.

But tomorrow, I'm going to practice my
dancing again. I will be ready to dance
again next May 5th!

Make Your Own Maracas

Music is an important part of Cinco de Mayo celebrations. Now you can make your own instruments and play along. Maracas have been used for hundreds of years. They are popular in Mexico and many other nearby countries.

What you will need:

2 disposable plastic bottles with their caps, such as water bottles (any size from 8 to 20 ounces)

uncooked rice or uncooked popcorn

masking tape

paint or markers

kitchen spoon

Directions:

1) Empty the bottles. Let them dry out completely. Remove as much of the labels as you can.

2) Drop uncooked rice or popcorn into each bottle. You will want to put about 4 spoonfuls into the first bottle. Put about 8 spoonfuls into the other bottle. Or try rice in one bottle and popcorn in the other. That way, the two will sound a little different.

3) Put the caps back on the bottles. Make sure they are tight!

4) Wrap pieces of masking tape around the bottles.

5) Decorate the masking tape with paint or markers in bright colors.

6) Let the paint or markers dry.

7) Pick up one maraca in each hand, and hold the maracas by the bottle caps.

8) Shake your maracas!

GLOSSARY

celebrate: to do something special to show that a day is important

Cinco de Mayo (SINK-oh day MY-oh): Spanish for the "5th of May"

costume: special clothing. People wear costumes to look like someone else or to look like they are from a different time or place.

instrument: something that you use to play music

maracas (mah-RAH-kahs): hollow instruments with small objects inside to make a rattling sound

mariachi (mar-ee-AH-chee): a kind of musical band that is popular in Mexico and parts of the United States

Mexican American: person living in the United States whose family originally came from Mexico

tortilla (tor-TEE-yah): a thin, flat, round bread

BOOKS

Cox, Judy. *Cinco de Mouse-O!* New York: Holiday House, 2010.
Join Mouse's exciting Cinco de Mayo adventure.

Hall, M. C. *Cinco de Mayo.* Vero Beach, FL: Rourke, 2011.
See lots of photos of Cinco de Mayo celebrations.

**Levy, Janice. Translated by Miguel Arisa. *Celebrate! It's Cinco de Mayo!:
!Celebramos! !Es el Cinco de Mayo!*** Park Ridge, IL: Albert Whitman, 2007.
Read in English and Spanish about a boy and his family celebrating Cinco de Mayo.

Lowery, Linda. *Cinco de Mayo.* Minneapolis: Millbrook Press, 2005.
Learn more about Cinco de Mayo and the history of the battle between the
Mexican and French armies.

WEBSITES

Click'N'Say Numbers
http://www.123teachme.com/games/click_n_say/numbers
This website from 123 Teach Me will teach you how to read and say
numbers in Spanish—including cinco!

Puzzles
http://www.jigzone.com/puzzles/1712004174C?z=6&m=A9C9000F
Try your skill at an online puzzle of the Mexican flag—just drag the pieces into place!

Sesame Street Cinco de Mayo segment
http://www.sesamestreet.org/video_player/-/pgpv/videoplayer/0/3fa430e4-188b-4efe-bb77
-b17ee6bb8615/cinco_de_mayo
Watch as these kids and families celebrate Cinco de Mayo with music and fun.

LERNER e SOURCE™
Expand learning beyond the printed book. Download free, complementary educational resources for this book from our website, www.lernerresource.com.